SEA CHANGE
DO CHANGE

FRANK DAPPAH

OSTRICH

Ostrich Press LLC. www.ostrichpress.com

Copyright © 2012 Ostrich press

All rights reserved.

ISBN: 9798722754752

DEDICATION

To my entire family for being extraordinarily supportive through all my endeavors.

To my wife and business partner, Bernice, for always having my back – through it all.

Thanks!

CONTENTS

	Introduction	i
1	Unchained Capital	1
2	Business as Usual	10
3	Breaking Down the JOBS Act.	16
4	Various Point of Entry	23
5	Flight Lessons	36
6	Life, Unboxed	47
7	Lightbulb Momentos	56
8	Printing Blueprints	68
9	Transubstantiation	78
10	Balancing Act	88
11	Open horizons	97

INTRODUCTION

Well, it looks like the boom times are finally here - For entrepreneurs and small business owners, at least. Never (after the dot com days) have I seen such a readiness and availability of cash to boost businesses.

Between the Federal Reserve's "easy money" policies, various COVID rescue plans passed by the United States Congress, and as result, folks just having more money in their pockets than things to do with it, there are currently more folks looking to throw cash at startup businesses than startups available to take said cash.

The extreme availability of liquidity in the markets has indeed helped hasten mankind's drive towards innovation.

As *Cathy Wood* of ARK Invest fame once put it once:

"COVID has created a lot of problems, and we are investing in companies that are working to help solve these problems".

This is the situation we find ourselves in now as a global community. We must make way and financially support the companies and the products that emerge to help humankind face the next 10, 20, 30 years.

You take all these moving parts and add on the fact that over the last five years or so, various (major) policy changes here in the U.S and the availability of the Internet, mobile technology, and social media, then you have the perfect storm to unleash, for better or worse, the power of capital.

Not just from major financial institutions, but from the everyday retail investor.

As I stated earlier, with just a business plan and a good idea, folks can now tap into virtually unlimited public capital. Much-needed capital to help bring said ideas to life.

With just a smartphone and a credit card, folks can now connect with entrepreneurs looking for capital to help build the next big thing. There have been major innovative companies - I am talking about well-known firms like Zenefits, the online H.R platform, and Robinhood, the preferred investing platform for today's investor, that initially raised capital from everyday folks via some of the various crowd equity portals out there. A little bit more on this topic later. It has become abundantly clear at this point that the world we knew pre-COVID is far behind us, and we will most likely never live in that world ever again. The good news is that the pandemic forced all of us to think deeply about the way we live our lives. To look closely at ways in which we, as a global community, can make better choices and *build back better* with the resources we already have available to us. Our current situation has also forced us to rethink income inequality, social equity, race-related issues, investing, energy production, and so on. So, what does this all mean, and how did we get here?

In the next few chapters, I shall chat with you a bit about various trends helping shape the world of Startup investing. I shall also discuss the various events that led to where we are today. And lastly, I shall share with you a few of the resources available, and strategies I think you can explore to perhaps tap into private capital for your Startup company or idea.

#ONE

UNCHAINED CAPITAL

Entrepreneurs make the world work. Or rather the companies and the products and services around which we build organizations move our species forward. I say so knowing for a fact that the universe of entrepreneurship and all that surround the conception-to-creation of new products is copiously familiar to even those that extend beyond the startup ecosystem.

What I am trying to say is, you clearly do not have to be one: an entrepreneur, to know about what these folks do. You probably could pick some notable names/faces like Zuckerberg, Gates, Buffett, out of a line up. There are media empires built only for the purpose of covering entrepreneurs and what they do.

Forbes, CNBC, Inc. Media, and so on. Not only do we buy what we need and want, we also spend a lot of time talking (about), thinking (about), and heaping praise on the men and women who start and run the firms that produce our favorite products and services.

For folks who start firms, or even think of starting firms - and succeed, we, as a society, often have no issues with giving up the spoils of success: Wealth, fame, reverence, and so on. And rightfully so, I guess.

I mean we can argue all day about whether the treatment of these men and women as superstars is healthy for our psyche of our society, and I for one would agree that we sometimes go too far in hailing those who succeed in launching companies as heroes.

Anyone among us can certainly make that argument. And various aspects of that thesis would be universal truths. We can even explore what it means to be a "company" and whether or not we sometimes allow the glitz and glamor to overshadow the fundamentals of some of the firms and the folks we hold up as "successful entrepreneurs" and "innovative companies". I for one believe that Peloton Interactive Inc. does not make any sense as a long-term viable organization. At least, not until the company finds a way to produce a product and/or service that adds value to their customers' lives and not have to hit them over the head with a $2000 price tag for what really amounts to a stationary bike with a big computer screen attached to it.

I think their (Peloton's) entire business model is based on a fad. I think, thanks to loosened regulation and excess capital, not to mention ease of raising said capital, there are too many Peloton's and Clover Health's in the marketplace.

We cannot, however, deny what a multi-dimensionally cumbersome balancing act it is to launch a new company.

There are many reasons why startup-ing (often) is so challenging. For one, you as the entrepreneur, will typically find yourself in a situation in which hitting your goals would be only possible with a myriad of things working well at the same time.

Beyond having an idea for a business or a product that you and your team think makes sense, you will need access to capital, a robust system via which you can test and launch your prototype or beta version of your offering, among many other steps. As we have talked about thus far: Access to capital is a bit more streamlined these days than it used to be. At least for the small -scale startup.

Investors everywhere
Unless you have been living under a rock or have been in a coma for the last six years or so, you have probably noticed an unusually large number of folks looking to invest their hard-earned cash to help back various types of Startups.

You probably will find out (if you asked) that a bunch of your friends, colleagues, and family members currently hold shares in a host of startup companies.

You most likely have also noticed more of the everyday folks looking for opportunities in private and public equity investments. Sure, the pandemic has fueled the rise of the retail investor. Truth be told, this trend has been about a decade in the making.

Folks, everyday folks, have longed for the days when they too could participate in deals previously only available to deep-pocketed families and financial institutions. Well, those days are behind us now, and these days, anyone can buy shares in their local favorite coffee shop, or bike repair shop. And the process is easy too.

Crowd surfing

It seems like, these days at least, that crowdsourcing has become the way to do all kinds of things. And rightfully so. There is enormous power in say, raising capital online from hundreds, or thousands of folks. In this case, not only does one get to accomplish the goal of obtaining capital to start or grow a business, but you as the entrepreneur/proprietor get to know whether there is a large enough demand out there for what you hope to offer.

I mean, it makes sense, right? A person willing to cut you a check to go out and start a company or to grow one must really think that what you have to offer makes sense. Or that there is a market for what you have to offer. By participating in this process: Raising startup capital via Crowd Equity platforms, you get a chance to absorb all the valuable feedback and insights you can get from your investors, followers, and so on. The benefit of Crowdfunding goes far beyond just access to cash, and I caution entrepreneurs against going into it with rigidity of mind and a lack or the ability to take feedback that might not be what one wants to hear.

The right crowd

If you were not already aware of their existence, then let me elaborate a bit on what Crowd Equity is and the platforms that facilitate these types of transactions.

<u>What is Equity crowdfunding?</u>
For the most part. Equity crowdfunding, or crowd-investing, allows small companies and startups to raise capital from the general public by offering shares or other types of securities in their companies. As a result, the entrepreneur gets the money they need to

build their business, and the investor gets a stake in the firm. In other situations, I have seen, some entrepreneurs will offer other types of deals. I have seen some types of transactions that function as debt instruments or warrants, allowing the investor to receive monthly payments and the option to convert one type of security to the other.

Keep in mind that, these types of deals have only been around for a few years. Sure, rich folks have long been able to make these deals, either directly or through Venture capital, Angel funds, and so on. But recent law changes make it possible for folks like you and me to also potentially wet our beaks via these types of transactions.

One of President Obama's last acts in office was to help pass the Jumpstart Our Business Startups Act (JOBS Act). Although, a big bulky bill, the law was meant to help grow the U.S economy via boosting startups.

So, as you would expect, there were many parts to the thing. The part that really led to what I call "unchained capital" is that part where rules around deals previously available to only accredited investors were changed a bit.

I will delve into the JOBS act a bit more in the next chapters. Feel free to skip the next two chapters if you already know what I am talking about here.

Anyway, so, these rule changes helped create the path for the rise of Equity crowdfunding portals like Republic (republic.co), Wefunder (wefunder.com), Equitynet (equitynet.com), and so on. Although, all these sites basically do the same thing: Bring entrepreneurs and investors together, there are differences in the types of companies they attract.

Republic, for example, is suited for firms that have had some traction. Perhaps your company has been around for a few years. You have tested the market, proven your concept, and are generating revenue. Maybe even profitable.

Republic is great to get your face out there and to raise funds. There are some deals on the site that are still only available to accredited investors, but most of their deals are open to the general investing public.

Wefunder, on the other hand, is great for startups of all kinds. I have seen folks with just an idea and business plan in-hand, raise hundreds of thousands of dollars to go out and try to make things happen. I will, at the end of this book, provide you with a list of some of the Crowd Equity portals out there that I have used to invest in various startups. I will also share my thoughts on various once out there.

#TWO

BUSINESS AS USUAL

We often hear many of the experts of our day, in finance, economics, monetary policy, and so on, try to explain the sudden rise in consumer activism. Particularly in the world of finance and investing. We have seen the effects, and the kind of power that a group of determined retail investors can have and what a loud voice they possess as it relates to the fate of their favorite brands, valuation of companies, and their ability to move markets.

It stands to reason that in the 21st century, we would look at, and relate to our world in ways never conceived. Ultimately, it would seem, at least, that innovative thinking, democratization of, well, everything, and equity would be the tip of the iceberg, albeit equally important starting points to solving some of the major complications that plague our species.

We knew, going into 2009, that if we were to try to prevent the calamitous, never prevented but often expected nauseating fluctuations in our financial markets and economies as a result, we would have to rethink finance, industry, and the flow and management of capital.

As we listen to folks like Mary Barra at General Motors (GM) vow to move her company in the direction of clean energy, it becomes clear that the distant future we thought of as kids – if you were born in the 60's,70's, or 80's, is upon us.

It has been a long way up if you ask me. The recovery was complete. Well, until COVID came along. We were well on our way back to the top. I also think it's no secret that the last administration was no friend to innovation. His team's rise to power brought about, here in the U.S, the anti-intellectual age of our time. But that is a story for another time.

GM CEO Mary Barra

Long recovery

Many economists predicted we would have to take major fundamental steps, especially in our financial systems, if we were to rid ourselves of the stench of the last economic storm of 2007/2008.

The man in the Oval office seemed to understand this. Major policy changes were needed. So, major policy changes we got.

Safe to say the U.S government threw everything it had in its toolbox at the problem. Money, for the most part. I think we all know the timeline. After sharp declines in asset values and heavy job losses, the U.S economy began to grow in mid-2009. This tepid growth was of course preceded by the enactment of policies such as the financial stabilization bill (TARP) and the American Recovery and Reinvestment Act.

If you were around back then, you heard a bunch of these policies with cute names being thrown around. And who can forget the many congressional hearings, news articles, and television pieces about the state of our economy.

Following an onslaught of rule changes, monetary policy amendments, and so on, the economy finally started growing again.

Average annual GDP growth stood at about 2.3 per cent leading into the final year of the Obama presidency.

The days of lying awake at night wondering if the company you worked for would be the next to go under. And having to do something strange for a little bit of gas money were finally behind us.

That is until COVID came along. But we will call that a "brief interruption".

A step further

By 2012, with the economy and the job market strengthening, but not at a fast enough pace, it was clear that more was needed. The recovery had been a long one.

Even with "Quantitative Easing" still in full effect, more had to be done to supercharge our economy. It would make sense to attack the issue from the bottom up. Sure, thus far, we had adopted a top-down approach - In the sense that we would give boat loads of cash to large corporations in the hopes that the cash would percolate through the entire system.

Of course, this was not the case. It never is. Reality was starring the administration in the eyes. Small businesses needed a boost.

The corporate titans were paying bonuses and executing stock buybacks. Actions, though effective, but restricted to a few. One more step was needed. And a long overdue one at that.

For years, small business owners and small investors had been asking for easing of some of the

barriers to entry that existed on both ends. The JOBS act, among others, would do just that.

President Barack Obama signs the Jumpstart Our Business Startups (JOBS) Act, which includes key initiatives the President proposed last fall to help small businesses and startups grow and create jobs, in the Rose Garden of the White House, April 5, 2012. (Official White House Photo by Pete Souza)

#THREE

BREAKING DOWN THE JOBS ACT

Throughout human history, more specifically in the last fifty years or so, there have been events that have caused all of us, to question, examine, and rethink some of the very pillars, norms, and socio-economic systems of our modern society.

The great depression, World War II, the great recession, and now COVID, are all examples of such change-making events. Of course, there have been other (more focused) events that have also brought about change. Or our desire to take a closer look at any underlying issue. The recent killing of George Floyd by a police officer comes to mind.

The last non-pandemic financial calamity that befell us forced us to deconstruct and reconstruct various long-held economic principles. Particularly in the often-esoteric areas of the flow of capital, financial regulation, and energy procurement.

It is now clear to us all that financial equity begets shared exponential growth of individual wealth. Which results in higher standards of living and an overall higher quality of life for all. I would not be completely off the mark if I postulated that most of Obama's tenure was spent trying to create some sort of foundation to try to address these very real problems.

It is also my belief, as I write this in early 2021, that the New Biden administration plans to pick up where the former president left things and try to get us closer to these goals.

Table of contents

I can run through the greatest hits: Healthcare reform, Lilly Ledbetter Fair Pay Act, Free trade agreements, Climate change (The Paris Agreement), and The Dodd–Frank Wall Street Reform and Consumer Protection Act. Atop the heap of financial regulations and economic policies came The Jumpstart Our Business Startups Act, or JOBS Act.

What is the JOBS Act?
In general, the JOBS Act, which passed in both houses of the U.S Congress with overwhelming bipartisan support and signed into law by then-president Barack Obama back in 2012, was meant to significantly increase funding for small businesses in the United States.

The JOBS act came as a final (Beta version) solution to an issue that had plagued the U.S economy even before the financial crisis of 08. But even more so as a result.

If at first, you don't succeed.
Congress, in an effort to encourage funding for small businesses, had passed several bills prior to the JOBS Act being signed as law. There was The Entrepreneur Access to Capital Act (H.R. 2930), which was

spearheaded by U.S. Representative (R), Patrick McHenry.

There were many other bills that took aim at the same issue: Making funding and opportunity available to small businesses and startup firms. Most felt that the government needed to rewrite some of the laws that governed the flow of investment capital to small businesses. For far too long, access to public capital, which is the lifeblood of the world's economies had been available to only a few deep-pocketed and/or well-connected firms.

Billing issues

For the most part, the JOBS act addressed the following specific issues by way of provisions within the bill:

I. Increase the number of both accredited and non-accredited shareholders a company can have until it is required to file reports with the Securities and Exchange Commission, thus making it a public company. The previous thresholds were assets of $10 million-plus and/or 500-plus shareholders. As a result of the JOBS Act, Small companies can now have up to 500 accredited shareholders or 2000 total shareholder before it is required to file with the SEC.

II. With an annual cap of $1,000,000 (for companies), restrictions on the use of the internet and equity crowdfunding sites were reworked in various ways. For one, the bill made it so that non-accredited investors, those with a net worth or annual income of less than $1 million, could participate in these types of offerings. Startups and small companies could raise capital via these platforms under less restrictive regulations. The government placed the reporting responsibility upon the shoulders of the equity crowdfunding portals and not on the small companies looking to raise capital. Normal folks could invest from 5% - 10% of their annual income if they are non-accredited. The bill mandated thorough financial reviews for firms looking to raise more than $100,000. As part of the push to make capital available to more companies, the bill also redefined "Emerging growth companies" as those with less than $1 billion in annual gross revenues.

III. The bill also allowed for general circulation or marketing of various private placement deals to non-accredited investors as long as such marketing efforts contain the appropriate disclosures and are based on confirmation from a third party.

IV. Raise the limit on private placement securities in general from $5 million to $50 million. This action was meant to allow smaller firms the wiggle room to have access to larger pools of funds without the cost-prohibitive aspects of having to register these deals with the various State and Federal regulatory bodies.

Crowdfund me!

Among the many other provisions in the bill are the

allowance of various types of Community banks to have up to 2000 shareholders. As opposed to the previous limit of 500. Investment funds and other types of registered money firms are prohibited from access investor capital via the use of crowdfunding.

In the next chapter, I shall take a closer look at The CROWDFUND Act. As I feel this is one of the more relevant aspects of the rule changes that affect access to capital today by small minority owned firms.

#FOUR

VARIOUS POINTS OF ENTRY

Depending on the proverbial waters in which you swim, you may hold significantly varying opinions as compared to others relative to whether you believe that startups today have access to (ample) capital at every level of the evolution of their companies, or not.

Although, I will point out that, as far as we have come in connecting everyday investor capital with entrepreneurs who so need said capital to build the next big thing, there is still much work to be done. That is a concession I think any progress-loving man, woman, or child will be willing to make.

It is incumbent upon our political, and business leaders to help go beyond the JOBS act to help create various mechanisms through which equitable opportunity and wealth can be realized through investing.

As it stands today, as a result of innovation, social media, and the democratization of information, there are various ways in which founders of startups and small businesses alike can connect with the right people to raise capital for their firms.

As we delve deeper into the various topics I wish to address in this book, I feel it is important to look at (first) the various pathways to raising public capital and the "suitability" factor for your firm.

To be perfectly clear, your growth as a firm will go a long way to determine which kind of mechanism will help you get the best out of your fundraising efforts.

Bridges and tunnels

If the current COVID pandemic has proven nothing at all, it has at least shown all of us how social we really are. Folks were having an extremely hard time staying isolated. Even for a few weeks. As much as we all pretend, we do not need one another, turns out we do. We, humans, are social creatures. Every aspect of our lives, or should I say the successful execution of every part of our lives, depends heavily on our ability to make meaningful connections with other human beings.

We must work hard to build healthy bonds with our friends, family, business partners, and so on. This is an all-important part of our happiness and overall mental health profile.

So, when it comes to getting yourself out there to raise capital for your firm, regardless of the seeming seamlessness of the process due to technology, you must still be able to get out there, in-person or virtually via Zoom, to pitch your idea/company.

This part of the process still has not changed. And the folks who have the greatest levels of success connecting with both older and newer investors do this very well.

It also pays to have a compelling product,

service, or idea to pitch. You must be able to get valuable introductions to folks looking for companies like yours to invest in and communicate with existing friends and acquaintances to help them understand the value of your proposition. That is if you initially raise capital from your own personal social circle.

From A to Z

Depending on the stage of evolution of your company, the size of your firm, your future plans for your organization, not all capital will be appropriate. If you, for example, want to set up a small barbershop.

One that you wish to keep small and local. A single-location-type of operation, going out to solicit $200k from 1000 investors might seem cool and easy, but might not be appropriate for your situation.

In these types of situations, it might be a good idea to consider first what you want this hypothetical barbershop to be, how you wish to "exit" the business down the line – do you want to one day leave it to your son or daughter? And the type of operation you wish to run. How profitable you hope to be, and if not, what your contingencies are and so forth.

My thinking is that one must get themselves ready for the ball if they wish to be invited to the big event.

First on the scene
Some things just never go out of style. Indeed, if you have an idea for a business or a product - One that is yet to be proven viable for any sizable market out there, and you need cash to build a prototype, Beta version of your app, and so on, it helps for you to dig deep into your own wallet to make that happen.

I know this seems counterintuitive but trust me when I say that you want to create a viable product or even a business first before going out and trying to raise outside capital.

The good thing about looking to build products and/or services in this new world order is that, apart from some niche types of industries, you can start wherever you are in life with as little cash as possible. If you are looking to start an eCommerce business, even if you hope to be the manufacturer and deliverer of some unique set of SKUs, you can always, using apps like Shopify and Inventory source, build a robust eCommerce site and find suppliers in your chosen category to source and deliver your offerings to your customers.

You can always find manufacturers – with new cash in-hand – to build your very own branded product line for you later in the game. You will at the very least have (cheaply) started your business, proven a market for what you offer, and be in the best position possible to pitch your new company to potential investors.

Knowing you can show plus signs on your balance sheet. And believe me when I tell you that as an investor of startups myself, me loves me some plus signs (on the balance sheet).

Folks like to invest in businesses, and not ideas. Every Tom, Dick, and Harry has an idea, and the only folks who will typically think that you have "a good idea" are going to be you, and your closest associates. And you, as an entrepreneur, can leverage this belief in yourself and others' expectations of you to raise the first-in type of capital you might need to get your idea off the ground.

Once this idea graduates from just being a fever dream you have. Once you are able to build a 1.0 version of your product, get your services business going, gain new customers, and so on, you will be able to attract cash from folks who invest in businesses for a living. You will also be in a good position to offer your investors a return on their equity in relatively short order.

Valuations and more

As your business matures beyond the initial stages of development. As you start to gain traction in the marketplace and start to reach some of the operational milestones you set for your firm, you will start to get to the point where you need some serious cash.

Well, serious enough that you typically will not have that kind of cash on you. That is… unless you are already loaded. But, if you are like the rest of us, you will need some form of capital infusion.

At this point, you will probably not be able to secure a major line of credit or small business loan. Anyway, I would not recommend this type of financing at this point. At this stage, you will want to consider raising public equity or at the very least, take a closer look at bringing in outside investors.

I will not bore you with the mundane details of ways to go about raising capital as I am sure you have some ideas. I will however outline some of the technical aspects of the process.

Knowing your ABCs

Beyond your family and friends, any potential investor you approach, whether face-to-face or online via equity crowdfunding, will want to support your business, sure., but they, private or institutional investor, will want something in return for the cash they hand you.

We have talked about this a little bit already. I bring it up to help drive this point home because it may seem like a no-brainer, but you will not believe how many entrepreneurs I have interacted with in one way or another who simply miss this point.

Folks will either want a piece of your firm so they can gain capital appreciation they can later exchange for more cash than they put into it or want you to pay some type of frequent payment to them in the form of royalty or interest and loan repayment.

That being said, you must then first seek a third-party valuation of your firm. Various accounting firms and some niche platforms can help you with this. You can also do your very own research online to help you determine what your firm could be worth based on comparing your business to other like businesses.

With valuation in-hand, if you will then seek to start the process to embark on typically three chapters of funding. It helps to visualize you having to go out to and raise funds in multiple rounds so you can prepare, not just you and your team, but also your investors.

Green shoots

As we discussed, your earliest type of funding will come from friends and close associates: Your inner circle. Entrepreneurs typically use this type of funding to help develop a business idea and more so to nail down some of the most basic parts of launching a new business.

I am talking about stuff like registering your business, building a website, forming a corporation with your State's Secretary of State, and even building a prototype of your products.

Some businesses never go beyond this stage. They typically just rely on the occasional infusion of cash from their close circle of friends/investors and the founding team's own cash. They do so till the business starts to turn a profit. At which point a sale or occasional distribution of dividends occurs. Most startups, on the other hand, will go on to bring in more investors.

Seed funding

Not to be confused with pre-seed money, seed funding typically takes the form of anywhere from $10k to $1million. Funds from this type of funding will typically be used to retain an official founding team who will then take steps to succinctly execute activities such as market research, preliminary marketing and sales efforts, developing a version two of your product and so on.

At this level, it is typical to see other types of

investors participate. The so-called "Angel Investor" comes into play here. These types of investors are often other successful business folk who invest their own cash in young promising startups for a piece of the pie.

Going beyond seed funding

The series A, as I am sure you have gathered by reading news headlines, often involves small venture capital firms like New Profit and Serena Ventures, advocacy groups and Angel Investors. Firms that have managed to work through some of their starting pains, carved out a consistent source of revenue, built a growing user base or customers, will often seek additional funding after the seed level.

Cash from a series A is often put to work to scale marketing efforts and other revenue-generating activities within your organization. The typical size at this stage is about $2 million to $15 million. Entrepreneurs are, at this point, encouraged to build a team of investor/advocates to help bring other similar investors to the table.

SEA CHANGE, DO CHANGE

As the process of raising capital and engaging with investors become more time-consuming, it helps to have a point person within your organization to carry out investor engagement as well as a lead investor. Equity Crowdfunding, Wefunder, allows for firms raising cash to designate a "lead investor".

In 2014, I launched Serena Ventures with the mission of giving opportunities to founders across an array of industries.

As your company expands and you start to find yourself making significant capital expenditures, ones that will often outpace revenue growth, you may look to raise additional funding in a series B, and C.

At these stages and subsequent funding

	Series B	Series C
Typical size:	$10 Million	$50 Million
Main investors:	• Venture capital firms • Investors from previous rounds • Select Angel investors	• Private equity firms • Large venture firms • Hedge funds • Banks
Uses of cash:	• Scaling customer base. • Growing paid operational team.	• Acquire other businesses • Develop new products and services • Move into new markets

rounds, you will start to engage with firms that come to the table much later in a startup's lifecycle.

You will start to generate interest from Investment banks who hope to get in for a return in the event of an IPO or a SPAC deal. Private equity and Venture arms of large banks like Goldman Sachs and UBS often get in on these types of rounds as the next step for a startup at this stage will be some kind of exit. See chart below for differences between both funding rounds.

#FIVE

FLIGHT LESSONS

Are there folks out there raising boatloads of cash

with just a business plan in-hand and a sleekly-design pitch deck? Sure, there are!

The thing though is that from the average investor standpoint, these are often very risky deals. Though, most cannot tell. Why? Because the everyday investor seems to (often) struggle to make the distinction between a startup business and an idea.

From your perspective, developing your product or service offering, and gaining traction, will help you protect yourself and avoid various potential, often realized cataclysmic outcomes. So, let me list just a few.

Valuation erosion
If or when you decide to go out there, whether via your own personal contacts, through professional introductions, or through one of the many equity crowdfunding platforms out there to raise money for your startup, you will have to ultimately strike some kind of deal with your investors in exchange for their funds.

These deals are typically on an equity basis, debt obligations, warrants, or a combination of more then one of these options. My point is you will have to provide a performance-based return in the form of capital appreciation or have to pay back funds borrowed with interest.

In most cases, the type of business you are engaged in will determine the route you take. In my experience, taking on debt at such an early stage in business may not be such a good idea as you will need all the free cashflow generated to grow your business.

Although, in most cases having some kind of service business is always ideal as these types of businesses tend to generate higher profit margins. Businesses like Software-as-a-service, financial services, consulting services, and so on.

These tend to provide the kind of net profit numbers that can allow one to pay down debt while maintaining healthy cash (reserves) levels.

Keep in mind that while no two businesses, or for that matter types of businesses are alike, in any situation you find yourself raising cash in, you will be able to attract more funds and a higher quality of investors if you have a business that, well, does business.

You stand a better chance obtaining higher valuations and as a result, not have to give up a chunk of your business if your business has:

- ❖ Paying customers

- ❖ An experienced management team.

- ❖ A reliable, replicable business model

- ❖ A sales team or strong marketing infrastructure

- ❖ Plans to 10x your revenue over the next 5 – 10 years.

- ❖ Makes a profit with growing profit margins.

These are just a few of the aspects of business that it helps to have acquired before you set out to raise capital. You do not have to have addressed every single one of these.

That is not what I am saying. It helps if you are much further along in your business than just "I have a great idea for a business". In the next chapter, I will delve into these aspects of traction a little bit more.

Chipotle Mexican Grill Inc

Growth (3-Year Annualized)

Revenue %	Operating Income %	Net Income %	Diluted EPS %
10.16	4.12	26.38	26.60

As of Dec 30, 2020

Profitability

Return on Assets %	Return on Equity %	Return on Invested Capital %	Net Margin %
6.42	19.21	7.27	5.94

As of Dec 30, 2020

Based on the most recent numbers from Morningstar, the popular Mexican eatery enjoys a healthy 5.94 % net profit margin. One of the best in the sector.

Intuit Inc

Growth (3-Year Annualized)

Revenue %	Operating Income %	Net Income %	Diluted EPS %
13.91	15.34	22.84	22.33

As of Jul 30, 2020

Profitability

Return on Assets %	Return on Equity %	Return on Invested Capital %	Net Margin %
24.76	44.31	31.88	25.10

As of Oct 30, 2020

Intuit on the other hand, a software company that has, over the last 5 years or so migrated completely to the cloud enjoys a nice 25.10% net profit margin.

Dilution of equity

Two things to consider here when discussing this point. Two things we can all agree on is the as you grow your business, especially if you have not quite figured out what you are doing yet, you will probably need to keep feeding your growing business cash. The other thing is that if you go the route of solely issuing stock for said cash, you will eventually run into the "equity dilution" conundrum.

While issuing more stock for a growing business is not such a bad thing, and you can always issue different classes of stock, you will want to minimize your equity float, so you retain more of your business for yourself and key employees.

It is hard to hit a moving target. It is even harder if you are not sure what the target is. Starting out in business usually feels like the latter.

For this reason, and others, it helps to first figure out some of the more basic aspects of your business before you start to raise capital. Your pre-seed capital should be used to expand on some of the aspects of your business that are revenue-positive and fundamental. Before heading out to bring in outside capital. This way, you have fewer equity offerings and avoid diluting the shares of your initial investors.

Defining equity dilution

Dilution occurs when a company issues new shares that result in a decrease in existing stockholders' ownership percentage of that company. Stock dilution can also occur when holders of stock options, such as company employees, or holders of other optionable securities exercise their options. When the number of shares outstanding increases, each existing stockholder owns a smaller, or diluted, percentage of the company, making each share less valuable.

Pre-Seed Funding

The earliest stage of funding a new company comes so early in the process that it is not generally included among the rounds of funding at all. Known as "pre-seed" funding, this stage typically refers to the period in which a company's founders are first getting their operations off the ground. The most common "pre-seed" funders are the founders themselves, as well as close friends, supporters and family. company founders themselves.

Lack of autonomy

A startup's ability to innovate is typically the main attraction. As you grow to become a "real company", you will inevitably lose this advantage. Even if you work extremely hard to try to maintain a corporate culture and overall ecosystem that inspires and nurtures innovation, you will see this advantage erode. This is just part of growing up as a business.

There will be many cooks in your proverbial kitchen. You will spend your days interfacing with both institutional and retail investors.

You will spend a great deal of time talking to lawyers, accountants and other professional consultants. Your days, if you are going to maintain your role as the CEO of your firm, will be filled with various mundane (but necessary) bureaucratic maneuvering.

Folks like Venture firm partners will weigh-in on every aspect of your operation. Though, these are all parts of running a business and it helps to have folks who advise you - especially folks with deep industry knowledge - it will be in your best interest to try to avoid these issues at the outset.

As you work to try to figure out what your business model will be, and more importantly what your strategy to grab market share will be, it is best to limit your decision-making systems to a few core folks, so you have the bandwidth to accomplish your initial goals. Once you have been able to determine product/market fit, acquired a few customers, and created a real business with repeatable systems, you may expand your team(s) as you see fit.

SEA CHANGE, DO CHANGE

#SIX

LIFE, UNBOXED

Democratized data dissemination, shared experiences, connectivity, and the pandemic have all lead to a need for innovation across all aspects of daily life. As entrepreneurs, we are best served to keep up with the new technologies and services shaping the way we do things going forward. All things. For, indeed, when COVID came to town, no one was spared. Not the rich nor the poor. Man, woman, child.

We have all had to adjust to the way we shop, eat, visit with friends, and work. I, myself, have gotten used to watching my favorite late-night shows with little-to-no audiences. I hate to admit it but I prefer Colbert all relaxed and taping his show from what I am assuming as an abandoned warehouse, with his wife Evie off to the side, laughing at some, but not all of his jokes - Almost like giving her stamp of approval to certain punchlines, but not others. In fact, you know the joke is (really) funny when Evie laughs audibly.

Stephen Colbert flirts with his wife Evie in cute 'role play' sketch

We have all had to shift gears is all I am saying. And by doing so, a whole new world of possibilities has opened up. Entrepreneurs around the world and investors alike must now be the engine the drives innovation. A reimagining of the world around us and how we interact with said world: Change!

The type of change that will help the rest of us navigate our new reality in a post-COVID-19 world.

In response to this daunting task, we are seeing major breakthroughs in the world of medicine, education, communication, and so on. I feel it is important to share with you some of these innovations as we discuss the world of startups and investing in startups.

My goal is to present these emerging fields to you so as to help set into motion some sort of freaky, creative chain reaction.

As early as March-April of 2020, when we were all getting acquainted with COVID. Around this time, we all suddenly realized that the best thing we could do to help slow the spread of this new virus was to create some space between ourselves and others.

Made sense, right? We did not know much about the new, more communicable strain of SARS. Other than the fact that spread seemed to be through droplets passed from person-to-person when in proximity. Lockdown orders were instituted across the world.

We all figured we would be away from work, and the rest of life for a few weeks. A (maybe) much-needed break for many. But by the summer of 2020, it was clear that this fight would not be as easily-won as we had all hoped – even anticipated.

And we would need to stay six feet apart for a little longer. This is when we started to take advantage of one of the already available tech innovations to help us stay productive, active, healthy, and in touch with the people that matter to us the most.

Zooming in

The use of video devices to communicate, I must admit, is nothing new. Since the likes of Skype, Facetime, and a few others hit the scene about a decade ago, some among us have been sharing our experiences with others in this highly visual way long before the pandemic hit.

I know many folks that insist on communicating via video. Something that annoys the heck out of me. If I am being honest.

Whether for business or personal use, folks

have been using video-based telecommunication technology for a while now. Even, the now ubiquitous Zoom is tech that has been around since 2011.

What has changed? Well, you do not need me to tell you.

Now, more so than ever, we must find new ways to use these technologies and build upon them to help us surmount the many challenges that stem from our need to put some distance between ourselves and others while still trying to maintain the normal processes of our daily lives. Upon the many technological advancements, we have made, we must find various ways to innovate to stay productive, healthy, happy, and so on.

Virtual wellness

I use this term to describe the emerging use of technology to connect individuals and groups to the wellness services they depend on. Telemedicine is one of the many mechanisms that first come to mind when speaking about virtual wellness. Although, firms like Teledoc, one of the first to innovate in the areas of medicine using teleconferencing technology, have been around for a while now.

Their services and others like it used to be a new curiosity. The idea, when they pitched to healthcare companies and workgroups was that using their platforms was to be viewed as an add-on to their already existing healthcare plans.

To employers, this was a way to save money on the cost of plan administration, among the many other costs associated with planning and executing an impactful group health plan. The idea was that their group members would be compelled to lean on the convenience of telehealth to help catch any potential health issues early. The use of telehealth would then save the plan sponsor tons of cash. Savings that could be passed on to the customer/patient/employee.

Now, telemedicine has become the primary way through which folks without serious medical concerns access primary healthcare. The technology and any other peripheral services have had to evolve quickly to support the sudden surge in demand.

We are also seeing the emergence of various

entrepreneurs around the world tapping into this new demand for telehealth technologies and services to roll out their own new ways to deal with not just the primary healthcare level but also mental health, oral health, and others.

Firms like Trusst, OTIS Dental, and Oracle Health, with their nimbler infrastructures and lower cost, will help drive down the cost of healthcare and lead to more options for consumers and untold opportunities for entrepreneurs around the world.

SEA CHANGE, DO CHANGE

Trusst is on a mission to transform the delivery of mental healthcare

At Trusst, we have assembled the national experts on messaging-based therapy to deliver an **empirically-validated, HIPAA-compliant app** that solves the scalability and affordability crisis in mental health care.

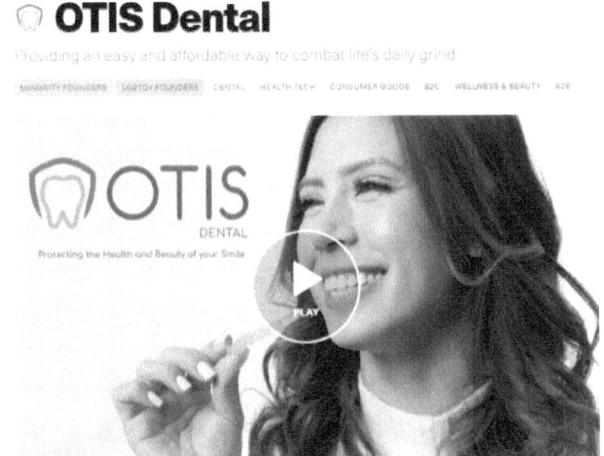

Doing the people's work

One of the often ignored but meaningful changes that has come about as a result of COVID has to do with the way governments around the world, elected to serve the people, now must conduct the business of their respective countries, States, cities, and towns.

During the COVID scare of 2020, even the world's collective judicial system was impacted. Here in the States, we saw various states decide to suspend all court proceedings. That is until it became clear that things were not going back to "normal" anytime soon.

Various territories had to find ways to return to the courtroom in ways that didn't involve actual bodies in the building. We also saw the United States Congress migrate to a semi-virtual model.

School systems around the country instituted an across-the-board virtual learning regiment. Believe it or not, out of this need for governments and other public institutions to stay "virtual" comes many small firms, started and run by entrepreneurs of all backgrounds, working on building the next generation of government processes.

#SEVEN

LIGHTBULB MOMENTOS

Imagine if I were to play a list of songs from back when you were a kid. Maybe jams from your high school days. Or even earlier than that. This is a timeline that belongs to only you. Your own special third dimension where moments, songs, emotions, events, all meet in a place in time specific to your very own unique experience. Sure, we all danced to Salt-n-Pepa's Push it but to you, this song might mean something else.

I bet every song I played in the hypothetical oldies' favorites playlist would conjure up visions of an exact event or set of events at that exact moment in your life. Something(s) that happened - good, bad, or otherwise but changed/shaped your life all the same.

Salt-N-Pepa: Push It (Video 1987)

And even these scenes fade from your mind's eye, as the years go by, hearing your favorite songs from back in the day brings back all those locked-away memories. Like most people, I do feel this way about music, movies, TV shows, and even companies.

For me, America Online, Hi5, Napster, and a few others serve as demarcation marks any time I embark on a review of my life. Those born in the early '80s know what I am talking about. AOL was all the rave back then and apps like LimeWire and a few others were our YouTube music.

I look around these days and I feel like for better or worse, we are reliving the tech boom of the mid-'90s - early-2000's all over again. Though the last runup ended badly for the general investing public in many respects, it also gave us iconic, enduring companies like eBay, Amazon, Microsoft, Skype, and many others.

Our last burst of innovation in this country and around the world was due to the popularization and proliferation of the world-wide-web. This time around, Coronavirus, 5G, the need for health and wellness services, and climate change are the reasons we find ourselves needing to roll out various technologies and solutions to help move the world forward.

That being said, I feel that no book about entrepreneurship, investing, and innovation would be complete if I were to skip the part where I share some of the firms out there, I feel are ramping up to provide the next crop of solutions to help define what life after 2020 will look like.

The Queen's gambit

Cathy Wood, CEO of ARK Investment Management LLC

Unless you have not been paying attention to the news at all in 2021, you know that the world of investing has been shaken up. Where we land next, nobody knows. What we do know is that as a result of all of us being locked up with a ton of cash from various stimulus programs and zero interest rates, a lot of us have delved into the world of investing.

Not just in public companies but also in private firms as well. We have talked about this already in earlier chapters of this book.

What folks are realizing now is the power to

collaborate with other investors on various social media platforms to help shape our investment decisions.

Like in any era, with any movement, the participants in said movement must find their oracles. The folks they look to for advice and guidance. I think folks from my timeline had Buffet, Mohamed A. El-Erian, and others.

Younger folks today have Cathy Wood and her Ark Invest investment management company. Cathy, a soft-spoken, forward-thinking 65-year-old (but looks like she is in her 40's) is notable for a few reasons.

For one, she uses social media more effectively than any other investment professional out there. She has a unique way of channeling enthusiasm for the firms her company invests in.

What makes her firm one of my favorites though is what they are doing over there at Ark. Working remotely with a crew of less than 30, Cathy has grown her assets under management to over $50 billion.

Cash she deploys to find and provide funding

for companies she believes will produce products and services that will aid in mankind's ability to navigate life in 2021 and beyond. Ark, through its various Exchange-traded funds, has made several high-dollar bets on companies like Tesla, Crispr Therapeutics, and Teledoc Health, to name a few. Focusing on areas such as Artificial Intelligence, Autonomous Vehicles, DNA Sequencing, Robotics, and others.

Frontline challenges

One of the most cumbersome areas of being in the health care business, especially for frontline workers is the difficulty that comes with being able to communicate with other healthcare professionals who care for your patient(s), and emergency health workers' access to vital private patient data.

As it stands now, folks in the healthcare space struggle to disseminate vital, life-saving data to those who respond to emergencies concerning the general patient population, while remaining HIPPA-compliant.

These are all problems and obstacles exacerbated as a result of COVID-19. Various innovative firms are currently looking for ways to navigate these very challenges.

One of the obvious standout firms, to me at least, is Vocera Communications Inc.

The San Jose, CA-based company is in the business of developing products and services that help eliminate errors and obstacles in the healthcare space and other mission-critical fields and roles. The firm was founded in 2000 and has ben able to introduce various wearable devices that help improve outcomes for both patients and emergency response workers.

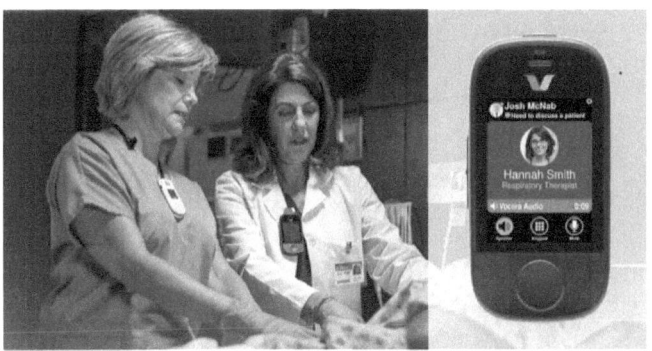

"The mission of Vocera Communications, Inc. is to simplify

and improve the lives of healthcare professionals and patients, while enabling hospitals to enhance quality of care and operational efficiency."

VR for your business

As we have discussed at great length, the way we live has changed since 2020. Changes I believe will remain (to some extent) for the foreseeable future. One generally-agreed-upon vital parts of our lives is our work. No matter who you are or where you live, if you are off a certain age, you probably do something for a living. How you do what you do has probably been impacted by Corona.

There are many workarounds found and been mined to aid you in earning a living going forward without exposing you to this virus and any others that will follow. One area being explored by firms like Pico is the use of Virtual reality and Augmented reality to help get work done.

The firm has developed a series of VR headsets that promise to bring our jobs to us in unparalleled realistic displays. Among the many features, their headsets boast:

- ❖ Six degrees of freedom tracking (6DOF)

- ❖ Room scale tracking technology

- ❖ True RGB Displays

- ❖ And much more

The firm intends to soon start to leverage its superior VR technology to help those working remotely to build a fully immersive work environment (virtually).

Meatlessness

Full disclosure: I am an investor in Moku Foods.

When I first found out about what they do, I was really impressed. I have never really considered myself one of those guys who suddenly "goes vegan" or tries some other trendy diet simply to save the environment. Or because everyone else is doing it.

I have never thought of going Keto, Pescatarian, Fruitarian, Lactovegetarian, none of the above.

I love meat. I used to be a straight-up steak and potatoes guy. That is until I hit my thirties. This is when the junk you eat ends up in all the wrong places on your body. It is usually all downhill from that point. And since I could not keep treating my body like a rest stop bathroom, I decided to start looking into other options. I enjoy the Beyond Meat products as well.

BEYOND MEATBALLS

Pre-formed and ready to cook, these plant-based me convenient, nutritious and satisfying addition to any me the meat aisle.

I sometimes head out into the countryside of North and South Carolina to meet with clients of my firm. These are the days I do the most junk food-ing. I started looking for healthy snacks. I asked around and I think someone sent me a link for Moku. I realized they were doing an equity round and invested.

So, what they do is basically turn Mushrooms into meat-flavored jerky snacks. That's it. Moku is a company built for the life ahead. They have a very light instructional footprint and efficient production values. Most of their customers swear by their products. I am convinced that, at some point, most food will be easy on our bodies as well as the environment. And companies like Beyond Meat and Moku foods are leading the way.

#EIGHT

PRINTING BLUEPRINTS

It is clear that for the sake of expediency, convenience, and the realistic expectation of success, one must have some idea of where one is going regardless of one's mission. And as unpredictable and as perilous as starting a new business may be, you, as an entrepreneur, owe it to yourself to immerse yourself in all the available resources to help ease - perhaps, even ensure- your way to success.

As I work towards the end of this book, with a couple of chapters left, I would like to use those two chapters to a) share some of the ways in which you can position yourself, your way of looking at things, and your company for success.

And b) share some of the resources I have found helpful when one embarks on the road to starting a business. Whether you have a goal of building your business to remain as a family asset, or you would like some kind of exit, it helps that even before you get started. Even before your first phone call to your first seed investor, that you take time to build a chronologically based strategy to start, grow, and exit your business.

Plans, pitches, and missions
Yes, I am talking about a good old-fashioned business plan. I mean it. I know it sounds outdated. And who can blame you and those who view having a detailed, living plan as some kind of antiquated practice?

Like home births. Or curing your headache with cocaine. I know it may feel this way because folks in the media keep telling you about all these folks who have built successful businesses with nothing but a few loosely scribbled words on the back of a dinner napkin. I am not sure about those guys and gals, but if you want to be able to build a business with a few hiccups, especially if you will take in outside capital, it helps to have some materials that will serve as a written, mutually-agreed-upon plan.

Here you want to include pitch decks and a basic business plan. You can look to apps like Canva and Liveplan to accomplish these two preliminary tasks. I will provide some (relevant) useful links in the next chapter.

Having a business plan, a stated mission and vision will also help CYA down the line as there will be no ambiguity of stated intentions. You can augment your plans later as your business evolves.

Just start with s basic plan if you are unsure as to where this idea of yours will go. Be sure to communicate the fluidity of your plans with all involved and come up with a systematic way to address any changes.

Making your mission all-encompassing will help you remain compliant with your overall intentions and also leave room to maneuver when needed.

The idea -to-business paradigm

Ask any active investor, Venture capitalist, or Angel investor and they will tell you that they, at this point in their careers, can spot a potentially successful business in three seconds. the thing is, no matter how unique your business idea is, there are certain things that you must be able to check off a list to be able to be a successful business.

I am talking about the kind of companies that can achieve exponential growth and even disrupt a sector. Quibi is an example of a product that did gain traction, but not enough to capture market share in the already crowded streaming space.

If you are not sure what Quibi is (was), Quibi was a short-form streaming platform built exclusively for mobile devices. The company later sold its content to Roku rather than be a stand-alone business model.

My point is, Quibi actually had great shows. I was unsure if there was a large enough addressable market to justify their existence. This brings me to the first steps in building-out your business idea to "take over the world". It helps to have a quick Q&A session with yourself and your team (if you have one at this point) to flesh-out your idea(s) a bit more.

Anna Kendrick befriends a sex doll in Quibi's show: Dummy.

Question #1:

Does your idea solve a problem?

This question must be taken on in two parallel ways. Solving a problem is the starting point of any great product or service. It also helps to know how bad this problem is for the folks who will spend money to solve said problem, and what type of folks they are.

Is this a problem they encounter during the course of

business? Or is this just an annoying issue they face in their daily (outside of the office) routine?

Is this a problem of the mind, heart, or wallet? In my experience, folks will pay top dollar for a solution to their money problems. The kind of issues that makes earning money harder. I personally never invest in consumer-facing software applications only because I am not smart enough to get the mechanics behind the process.

Question #2

What is your product or service, specifically?
This is where you, my friend, need to be as specific as possible. Feel free to document the minutia of your offering. You will want to be able to address this topic in a way that will make sense from an operational point of view.

It is one thing to say "we offer accounting services to small businesses" and a totally different thing to spell out what types of accounting services. Will you offer basic book-keeping or offer tax prep, payroll, etc.

Will you deliver your services via some type of software application or via human-to-human contact? Will you hire third parties to deliver the actual services while you serve as a broker or marketplace provider, or will you go out and hire a team to provide the services so they can hold themselves out as part of your organization.

Keep in mind that based on these two structures, one is a software play while the other is an actual accounting firm. Either comes with its own set of challenges and opportunities. What are some of the advantages your company will have? Will you try to take market share via offering value, or service? These are ways to try to map out the specifics of your product or service offering.

Question #3:

Who are your competitors?

As you work your way through the specifics of your offering, you will naturally touch on two other important factors: Your competition and your business model. You might not have a complete picture of either at this point. That's ok, time and research will help you figure out both.

Do not assume that you have no competitors simply because you see no direct competition. You might have indirect ones. These are companies that in some other way solve the problem your potential market has in some ad-hoc way.

You will also want to identify the most dangerous competitor of all: The potential one. This type of ambush predator is even more deadly if they have a size advantage. I will give you an example: It would take Netflix over seven years to hit 73 million paying subscribers. A status Disney would hit and surpass in under 2 years. Why? because Disney possesses the economic advantage over Netflix.

Now suddenly, Netflix has a huge competitor, at a

time when the popular streaming service's operatonal growth is being weighed down by debt. Disney, despite its $58 billion debt also has $17 billion in cash. Cash that can be used to vastly grow their Disney+ brand abroad. Do not underestimate the power of the sleeping giant. Rather have a plan to address such an issue and communicate these plans as part of your pitch to investors, vendors, and partners.

Question #4:

The "addressable market" question

Once you know there are folks out there who have to deal with an issue all day long - perhaps you even happen to be one of those poor souls dealing with such an issue - you will want to try to see how many other folks have similar issue(s).

There are many tools out there online that can help you determine how large your target market is. Here, at this stage, you will not want to take any shortcuts. Do not just do a quick online search for some topline number to throw out at potential investors:

"The addressable market is $50 billion".

" We are looking at an addressable market of over 30 million people in the U.S alone".

Sure, these statements sound great but represent nothing other than what folks say in crowded conference rooms, or on Zoom (pitch) calls. I challenge you to dig deep beyond the stated numbers and try to understand, on a molecular level, who this market encompasses.

Who is your ideal customer, where do they spend their dollars, how are they solving their issue now? How do you plan to connect with them and demonstrate value? and so on.

#NINE

TRANSUBSTANTIATION

Once you work your way through some of these (generally-inquired-about) points and you are confident that you have a winning business idea on your hands. I personally try to go out and prove my thesis.

This can be done by approaching some of your ideal customers to see if a large enough number will pay for your specific product to solve their specific problem. If you are in a position to do so, gather as much intel from these potential users as you can. In most cases, as I said, if you can organize some kind of focus group, free wine tasting, popup store, etc. you will have placed yourself in a prime position to absorb as much intel about those you hope to serve as possible. With the right setting, circumstances, and offer, folks who might be ideal customers for your new idea/company will not hold back.

They will help you improve upon your idea as well as give you a clearer picture of pricing, product design, marketing verbiage, strategy, and so on.

For example, if you plan to provide a service to folks over the age of 60 in a certain geography, and during your focus group session(s), you find out that when you asked for an email address to follow up, most stated that they barely use the Internet, then you can go ahead, at this cash-strapped point, and scratch "Online advertising" off your list of ad channels.

At least when it comes to that part of the country - for now. Take notes. Embrace all feedback as these will help streamline your product or service, as well as how your company will be structured and run.

If you are not in a position to go out and get

this intel, fret not. You will be able to address this point once you have been able to build some basic form of your company and business. To do so - build your company - I want you to position yourself with the following in mind.

In my experience, although these may seem mundane and as a result often go unaddressed in most startup scenarios, these are vital to being able to run your firm smoothly, stay on the right side of your profit and loss statements, and avoid any operational and legal issues down the line.

Human capital

It may come as no surprise to you if you have ever been involved in a startup that "people" can and often make or break a company. I mean, even if you have never started a firm before, surely, you have worked and quit a position before, right?

In most cases, you did not necessarily have an issue with the company's products, or their employment of tactics that were unsafe for the environment, right? It was the people at that darn company. Was it not? It is vital - the most vital of all points - to bring on the right people very early on.

Human capital should be treated as the most important asset of all. Though this is not a line item on a company's balance sheet. Its investment in the right people is extremely consequential. it is therefore of the utmost importance that you bring on folks with the right experience, education, contacts, and most importantly, mindset to help you transform your idea into a profitable business.

Please refrain from the tried and failed tendency for entrepreneurs to fill positions with folks whose only qualification is that they are friends of the founder(s). Unless your buddy has the right experience or expertise and has his head on straight, take the time to seek out and partner with forward-thinking, experienced individuals beyond your own circle.

Your organization is only as good as its human capital: The top leadership, salespeople, middle management, and so on.

As an investor, this is the number one thing I

look at when evaluating a private or public company. In the absence of a track record, the investment community seeks estimates in the value of a startup's human capital. Specifically, the founding team's ability to execute their strategy, both in the long and short term. Sure, having a great product or service is, well, great. But can you deliver said product to the marketplace with the team you have? That's the real question.

Leadership from the top

Although leadership styles may vary, there are some commonalities that remain, well, common when evaluating the end-results of most management systems.

Flat-Earthers

There are those who favor a more decentralized, flat management style. Leaving decision-making authorities to those team members who have enough real-time operational intel to make the right calls.

Startup companies typically favor this type of management system. So do more established firms like Costco, the national discount store brand. Costco groups their management teams based on corporate divisions as well as store locations.

Each division enjoys autonomous decision-making. What this means is that all things being equal, the manager at your local Costco has the authority to carry your AI-powered Yoyo if she wanted to.

Flat management systems serve as a tool to help empower all employees to take responsibility for all aspects of the business. And to be able to independently make vital decisions when they need to.

Flat organizational structures eliminate any type of hierarchical mechanisms, leaving those on the frontlines room to do what they see as being in the best interest of the company, its investors, and employees.

Reaping the benefits of a flat management style.
Some of the many benefits of structuring your startup company in a way that employs all those you work with to operate in a free and almost independent way

are as follows:

- Strong team spirit and collaboration between all

- Exceptional customer service

- Your company's ability to stay nimble and make big changes fast

- Solutions-based team members

- High team morale

- Many more

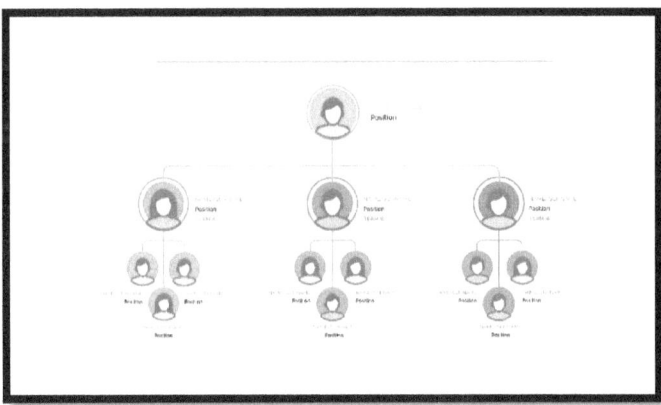

Flat organizational structure

There are those who believe that a central, top-down

approach to management is best for their organizations. Regardless of which suits your fancy, you must know that as the leader of a new organization, you must command control of, and responsibility for your entire infant team and their actions.

As a result, I believe that all CEO's, especially Startup chiefs must:

- ❖ Be detail-oriented and exhibit a hands-on interest in the day-to-day operating of their businesses.
- ❖ Know their work: Your team, especially those tasked to go out and sell your products and services must know that you could do it yourself if you needed to. When I ran a sales team, I made sure to spend most of my days with the team. This type of aptitude helps maintain high morale with the troops. And trust me when I tell you that your sales team is the most vital of all teams.
- ❖ Be great communicators: Your relationship

with your team should be treated with the care and attention exhibited in all your other relationships. Be mindful of the fact that folks need a positive, inclusive, work environment to be at their best. And their best is what will be needed to build this organization. Go out of your way to maintain positive, open lines of communication with your team.

❖ Work hard to keep drama at bay: While getting to know each other and working together, it is normal for personal issues to come up. Some issues will be run-of-the-mill stuff that typically work themselves out. Others might be the ones that pose a real threat to your company. Since you probably will not have an HR department when you start out, do your best to come up with a system to identify either type of issue, and how to deal with it. Designate one member of your team or even an outside consultant like a lawyer to help navigate some of these issues while you and your team work on your core mission.

❖ Eye on the prize: "I am not even sure what the point of this business is" is a question I have far too often found myself asking while working with many startup companies. The thing I have come to learn is that we all start out with a goal, no matter what we are doing. And if we are not mindful, end up in a strange place where building a profitable business seems to take a backseat to all the other issues folks find themselves preoccupied with. I Implore you to maintain a goal-oriented startup environment. The type of environment in which all folks spend most of their days working to improve the economic prospects of your organization. And nothing else.

#TEN

BALANCING ACT

Let me share a secret with you: Your business has more potential than you might think. And there are ways to build value in your company from day one. In small business circles, there is not a whole lot of emphasis placed on the metrics that help define a business and evaluate the effectiveness of a management team.

Larger corporations do a much better job at measuring success and maintaining a healthy balance sheet through various business lifecycles. When you embark on launching a business, as you get into the nitty-gritty of communicating with employees, customers, investors, and so on, it is easy to get lost in the daily grind. Most small business owners and entrepreneurs typically have a very one-dimensional way of looking at their companies.

Note that your business is what your organization does to generate revenue. Your company, however, is the entity through which you generate said revenue via one, two, three or more businesses.

For example, Warrant Buffet, through his holding company, Berkshire Hathaway is generally in the business of selling insurance products. Berkshire, however, operates various businesses. Some, wholly owned, while others are simply investments.

The firm, though most may not realize, generates most of its profits from its stock holdings. Mostly via capital appreciation, ahem, Apple! And dividend income.

Your firm needs to be looked at in a way that tackles various aspects of your capital, business model and so forth, to help you extract maximum value out of all your resources.

Return on everything.

This is a mantra I live by (as an entrepreneur). I am constantly looking for ways to extract ROI out of all company assets and resources. On your balance sheet sit many of your resources and encumbrances. Every business owner, I believe, owes it to themselves and their investors to always be on the lookout for ways in which one can eliminate debt while generating maximum return on their hard assets, intellectual property, and so forth.

We often, as small business owners, pay too much attention to our income statements. And not enough to the assets and liabilities of our organizations.

Most small operators I know, for example, have no Long-term investments as part of their hunt for profits and fight against inflation. Folks like Elon Musk and Warren Buffett have, over the years, made tons of cash for their shareholder, not just by building their businesses, but also via investing in other firms and asset classes.

Elon, for example, announced recently that Tesla had taking a $1.5 billion position in Bitcoin as a way to preserve balance sheet integrity.

A holding, we all assumed was procured for the average price-per-coin of $45,000 or less. We can safely assume that Tesla has thus far, made a nice little profit since Bitcoin is trading at $61,000 at the time of writing this book.

At my company, we too, at that time, had looked at Bitcoin and the entire crypto universe enough to also take a position via the excess resources available in our corporate cash accounts. What I am saying is that your cash reserves, for example, could be earning a return when invested (long-term) in stable, blue chip firms. In most cases, you can implement this strategy as part of your overall business model.

Do you have a full-time graphic design, or software development team? Well, you could roll out a service to help build websites and software applications. For other small business owners to generate income for your firm. Do you have expensive equipment that will not be used for the foreseeable future? There are times when your bottom line can be helped greatly by selling these types of non-performing assets to either pay a dividend to your investors or pay down debt.

Rethinking revenue

Please do not get me wrong or think I am being cynical when I tell you that businesses only exist to make money. Period. Sure, firms like PayPal, American Express, and a few others are notorious for investing in social issues and other projects these firms view as tantamount their core corporate operations - This is true.

Especially in these times when we have all been painfully reminded of some of the long-ignored issues that continue to plague our communities.

At the end of the day though, Paypal does not ignore its business to focus on social justice, or voting rights, and other special interests.

As an entrepreneur – and if you are reading this book, I assume you have outside investors or are thinking about raising capital – you owe it to all shareholders to be completely focused on creating shareholder value. And shareholder value starts with revenue. First comes revs, then gross profit, and so on. So, you, my friend, must take an out-of-the-box approach to revenue.

I have mentioned a few ways to generate cash for your firm, outside of your core business operations. If you are in the process of writing out a business plan or some kind of proposal - even as you proceed to file paperwork with your local government to officially establish your business, be sure to write out all the (peripheral) ways you think your firm can generate revenue.

During the worst parts of the pandemic, my company, like most firms, had to shut down some of our operations.

We leaned into our long-term investments and in those months generated more revenue from these stock holdings than any other part of our business.

I encourage you to think about all the many ways your company can make money. You can make money via **Joint ventures, Foreign currency hedging strategies**, by **marketing other firms' products and services, via renting out unused real estate assets**, and so much more.

Capital Infrastructure

I am always thinking about our capital infrastructure as a company. I spend a great deal of time backtesting and stress testing our balance sheet. I go beyond the recommended six-month benchmark and try to maintain enough cash to pay the bills and keep operations going for 1-3 years in times of crisis.

In all honesty, we only have one part of our business that does not generate revenue on a recurring basis.

And this part brings in the least amount of cash on an annual basis. This was by design. More like serendipity if I am being honest.

But that is not what I want to talk to you about. Your company should be built to last. Whether in good times or bad, you should build a system in which all sources of cash are tapped and ready, should you need it. It is important to take advantage of low interest revolving credit lines from your bank, government grants that can be used to build core parts of your business, and so on.

I personally think that besides Facebook and maybe Youtube, you should have grants.gov as one of your frequently visited websites. You should also retain as much of your investor capital as you can. Building this ecosystem should be something that you spend a lot of time on.

Most entrepreneurs ignore this and rather focus on the day-to-day of their businesses. And this is great… but all too often, we hear of firms that raise tons of cash from Venture firms, and Angel investors, only to go belly-up because they failed to attract additional funding.

You should build your organization to stand the test of time (from day one). And this can be done by, like I said, focusing on setting up various sources of funding (beyond cash from investors), keeping a healthy balance sheet, investing excess capital or allocating a portion of funds to be held in securities of other firms and alternative asset classes.

Try not to make fundraising a fulltime job, and work on being profitable from the outset. You can always innovate as you go along. These are some of the ways in which you can build a profitable business, while positioning your organization for the new business environment that lies ahead.

#ELEVEN

OPEN HORIZONS

During the course of this little book of mine, I have tried to discuss (in detail), a great many topics. Topics I felt would be of some interest to both watchers and participants of all things innovation, business, and entrepreneurship.

I will continue to write about these and other topics as time goes on. I am always interested in new trends and technologies that threaten to disrupt existing methods.

My goal in this very last chapter is to circle back and talk broadly about some of the trends emerging in all relevant aspects and to, as promised, share with you, some of the resources related to these topics. As we all brace ourselves in anticipation of what life will look like in 2021 and beyond. As we anticipate what life will look like once we are vaccinated and allowed back into the wild again.

As one would imagine, life will not be the same as it was in the before times. Some of the folks I know are now more than ever, focused on work, business, and life in general.

Most innovative folks I know are on the hunt for opportunities in ways to support mankind as we emerge from this horrid affliction known as COVID-A9.

That being said, look no further than these areas for inspiration:

Autonomous Driving technology

At this point in human history, there can be no doubt that while we retain most of the ways of doing things from a time long gone, there are various areas in which we have come to embrace innovation. One of these areas of rapid adoption and innovation is

Autonomous driving. Enormous levels of progress have been made in the quest to mature and deliver this technological platform to both consumers and the business community.

There are various verticals that stand to benefit immensely from Autonomous driving technology: Logistics, mail delivery, emergency response operations, and many others. As a result of the Corona Virus, consumers and business owners who previously viewed autonomous driving with skepticism are now looking at this shift more favorably.

According to The Consumer Technology Association, 26% of U.S consumers view autonomous delivery technologies more favorably than before the coronavirus health crisis.

Autonomous driving companies with permits to test their cars with a safety driver in CA reported 2.9 million miles driven. Aptiv and Lyft (combined) provided 100,000 'robotaxi' rides in the Las Vegas area.

Over half of small business owners believe their fleets will be 100% autonomous within 20 years.

These are but a few of the trends that clearly show our desire, as a global community, to make autonomous driving technology part of our everyday lives going forward.

Related reading

2030 The Driverless World: Business Transformation from Autonomous Vehicles

Life As A Passenger: How Driverless Cars Will Change The World 1st Edition

Artificial Intelligence, Robotics and connected technology

As most of America and the world return to work in 2021, we expect to see an exponential increase in demand for Artificial intelligence and Robotics, both in the lives of average folk and in the context of industrial applications.

There is an expectation of (particularly) supply chain and logistics operator needs. This expectation stems from languishing unemployment numbers, health risks associated with returning to work, and others.

Companies like Canada-based, Kindred Systems, and Vicarious are some of the firms expected to deploy various AI-powered solutions to help bridge the gap between workforce needs and supply.

Various startup firms are currently working on a myriad of solutions in the areas of robotics and internet of things to help power the needs of small businesses and other areas left unmet as a result of the pandemic.

As entrepreneurs, especially those who work with other businesses, I feel these are the times when no idea is a bad one. One must start to think of ways to implement (via various open platforms and partnerships) some of these solutions to help open new areas of revenue growth.

Covariant

Fast, precise singulation and accurate placement built for unforgiving environments

Covariant (covariant.ai/solutions), a U.S-based firm, designs and deploys various robotics and AI solutions to help reduce capex for small businesses in the areas of eCommerce, retail, healthcare and food service. The firm offers robotics solutions to fill service lines roles, order picking and packing and various others.

Vicarious

Kitting

Palletizing

Machine Tending

Vicarious (vicarious.com/solutions) offers, among other AI and Robotics solutions, Robot-as-a-service offer to help small businesses deploy advanced solutions at a fraction of the cost and time needed to build solutions from the ground up.

By design

Whether you are looking to build your very own product offering in this area, or looking for solutions to help power your business, you are able to glean inspiration by doing a deep dive into firms like these and connecting with folks who, like you, are deeply involved in the development, use, and research of AI and robotics.

By the numbers

- ✓ The AI, robotics, and IoT market is expected to grow to $15 trillion by 2030.

- ✓ The number of organizations using AI technology grew by over 200% between 2015-2020. Over 40% of organizations in 2020 use some form of Artificial intelligence solution.

- ✓ It is expected that by 2025, some sort of cognitive technology will have replaced over 16% of the U.S workforce.

- ✓ Areas in which AI and robotics are expected to have the most impact are healthcare, financial services, manufacturing, and telecom.

- ✓ Specific work roles in which AI, robotics, and IoT will be most needed will be in sales and marketing, customer service, and security.

Reimaging education: Virtual learning goes mainstream.

The Education sector is probably one of the areas of daily life most impacted by the pandemic. As economies around the world shut down in 2020, so did almost all private and public schools.

Most parents and students suddenly found themselves in the difficult position of having to endure the havoc caused by the virus in other aspects of life, while learning to continue schoolwork (support those who have to do school) from home.

There were various colleges in North Carolina and other areas of the country that tried to keep students on campus during this time - Only to later realize that "remote" was the only option, with everything that was going on.

As a result of this shift, there was a sudden need for software applications and tools that would enable student s to attend classes virtually. Some schools built custom solutions, while others tried to piece solutions together using apps like Zoom, and

Skype.

As we all realized that the shutdowns would last longer than first anticipated, there was a great need (and still is) for solutions that are built specifically to accommodate all the unique needs of education-from-home.

Firms like Blue Jeans (Verizon) and tandem are some of the newer solutions in the vertical. These outfits have built their offerings with the new dynamics of work and school in mind.

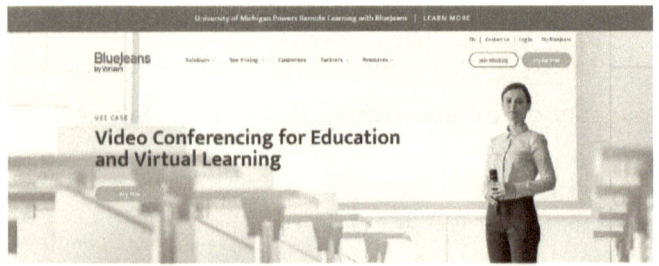

Engage Students with Virtual Learning Powered by BlueJeans

Instantly extend the boundaries of your virtual classroom with an immersive and interactive video conferencing experience that ensures faculty and students stay in sync, even if they aren't in the same physical space. BlueJeans provides a rich set of distance learning features that eliminate distractions, boost note-taking abilities, and improve group discussion to ensure that the virtual classroom is as effective of a learning environment as possible.

https://www.bluejeans.com/use-cases/education

Figma, a San Francisco, California -based organization helps educators and students connect in a more natural way to offer the most suitable experiences around. The firm, founded in 2016, has thus far raised over $100 million from well-known venture firms like Andreessen Horowitz, to help shore-up its application.

Experts expect the need for virtual learning and remote work solutions to only grow going forward. This new need leaves plenty of room for new entrants into the marketplace.

Contactless delivery and new-age logistics
Contactless delivery services have become extremely popular (for very obvious reasons). Since the pandemic hit, folks all over the globe have become all too familiar with the practice of taking delivery of all types of products while practicing social distancing.

A trend that is expected to continue, leading to the need for newer technologies that support the new paradigm of logistics. It is estimated that in the U.S alone, there has been a 20% increase in preference for contactless delivery options over the last year. This need spans many industries with hospitality in the lead. Outfits like DoorDash and Instacart have all migrated to a greater reliance on contactless delivery due to increased customer demand.

As demand for contactless delivery grows, so does the need for entrepreneurs around the word to innovate to fill said demand. Most new entrants into the space are improving outcomes and setting up to take on entrenched solution providers by further limiting the need for human intervention. More so than current options.

During the height of the pandemic, China-based, Meituan, helped local restaurants and other essential service providers deliver products to customers via the use of autonomous vehicles.

Here in the United States, outfits like Starship Technologies, and Manna are working to further incorporate the use of AI and other cognitive

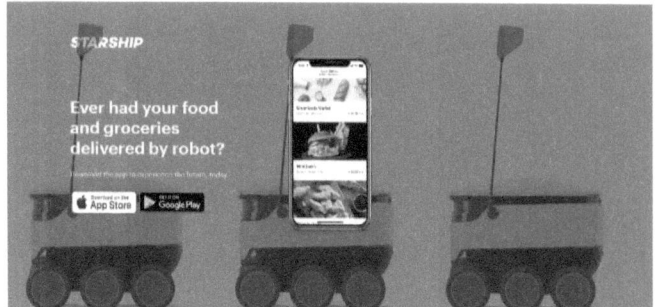

technology to help manage various areas of consumer-facing logistics, while keeping existing safety protocols in-play.

Starship Technologies

Starship, a San Francisco CA-based tech upstart promises to provide consumers with a completely contactless delivery experience. The services, currently testing in select cities, partners with local shops and restaurants to help deliver groceries and other items to customers' door by use of completely autonomous robots. The 6-year-old firm has raised some $90 million in funding since inception and is backed by various notable venture firms such as Morpheus Ventures.

To the moon

I say this all the time to everyone I know: "We are alive during one of the most interesting times in human history". Never before have we witnessed such huge changes occurring in the way we live.

The global availability of information, software application, robotics and many more, have all come together to create such great potential for those who aspire to build life-changing tools, products and services to live up to their greatest version of themselves.

Writing this book was something I felt was needed. Since We've all been cooped up in apartments condos, mansions, and villas, I felt the need to put some of the thoughts I was having on paper.

I typically write books about business,

marketing, e-commerce, and so on.

I feel that any entrepreneur living in these times, has available to them, great potential to build all sorts of interesting products and services - seeing that the pandemic has left us all looking at life a little bit differently - moving forward.

We would need folks with great ideas, big dreams and aspirations to help guide us forward.

life will never be the same. I think, at this point, we can all say those words with total conviction. However, what we do, Next is entirely up to us.

"Sea change do change" is my way of putting out some of my ideas.

Goodbye and good luck

I hope you enjoyed this, often meandering, hopefully informational book of mine. My purpose for writing this book – as I am sure we are all thinking about how COVID has changed our lives – was to help share some of my thoughts on the current state of things and discuss some of the many opportunities I see available as a result of some of the things we have been through in the last year. Stay safe, and God bless you and yours.

Thank you for buying my book!

SEA CHANGE, DO CHANGE

NOTES

https://www.cbpp.org/research/economy/chart-book-tracking-the-post-great-recession-economy#:~:text=Economic%20growth%20averaged%202.3%20percent%20per%20from%20mid%2D2009%20through%202019.&text=The%20Trump%20Administration%20projected%20that,discuss%20below%20in%20Part%20III

https://republic.co/about

https://www.bankofengland.co.uk/monetary-policy/quantitative-easing#:~:text=Quantitative%20easing%20is%20a%20tool,money%20directly%20into%20the%20economy.&text=Quantitative%20easing%20involves%20us%20creating,these%20are%20the%20same%20thing.

https://obamawhitehouse.archives.gov/blog/2012/04/05/jobs-act-encouraging-startups-supporting-small-businesses

https://en.wikipedia.org/wiki/Jumpstart_Our_Business_Startups_Act#Legislative_history

https://www.wsoctv.com/news/local/rallies-vigils-honor-george-floyd-charlotte-area/SVVHICFYSVGEBL3VNLCIWTC7XU/

https://mchenry.house.gov/crowdfunding/#:~:text=2930)%20was%20introduced%20to%20foster,stake%20(securities)%20to%20investors.

https://www.merchantmaverick.com/best-equity-crowdfunding-sites/

https://econsultancy.com/the-crowdfund-act-everything-you-need-to-know/

https://www.shopify.com/pricing

https://www.inventorysource.com/dropshippers/

https://www.investopedia.com/terms/d/dilution.asp

https://www.investopedia.com/articles/personal-finance/102015/series-b-c-funding-what-it-all-means-and-how-it-works.asp

https://www.serenaventures.com/

https://www.startups.com/library/expert-advice/series-funding-a-b-c-d-e#:~:text=A%20Series%20B%20round%20is%20usu ally%20between%20%247%20million%20and,who%20led%20the%20previous%20round.

https://www.lighthome.in/entertainment/hollywood/stephen-colbert-flirts-with-his-wife-evie-in-cute-role-play-sketch/

https://time.com/collection/best-inventions-2020/5911320/krisp/

https://republic.co/trusst?utm_campaign=trusst&utm_medium=rep_banner&utm_source=trusst_website

https://www.globenewswire.com/news-release/2020/08/25/2083421/0/en/Top-21-Founders-Changing-The-Way-We-Do-Business-in-2021.html

https://www.fastcompany.com/most-innovative-companies/2019

https://www.fastcompany.com/company/unity-technologies

https://time.com/collection/best-inventions-2020/

https://www.timeforkids.com/g2/best-inventions-2020-2/

https://www.vocera.com/vocera-smartbadge

https://www.pico-interactive.com/us/neo2.html

https://www.marketing91.com/flat-organizational-structure/

https://mokufoods.com/?gclid=CjwKCAiA4rGCBhAQEiwAelVti3d4OeYBAzISnjgaW_PfBLIWw2AUdMWMcqLLmBUzPADjWfKHDgFZ8hoCXsIQAvD_BwE
https://www.beyondmeat.com/products/

https://www.liveplan.com/how-it-works

https://www.canva.com/features/

https://ew.com/tv/anna-kendrick-befriends-sex-doll-dummy-trailer-quibi/

https://www.grants.gov/web/grants/search-grants.html

https://www.inc.com/anis-uzzaman/top-business-technology-trends-in-2021.html#:~:text=Trend%207%3A%20A.I.%2C%20robotics%2C,A.I.)%20and%20industrial%20automation%20technology.

https://www.cta.tech/Resources/Newsroom/Media-Releases/2020/June/Consumer-Excitement-for-Drones,-Self-Driving-Vehic

https://www.dmv.ca.gov/portal/dmv/detail/pubs/newsrel/2020/2020_08

https://www.amazon.com/2030-Driverless-World-Transformation-Autonomous/dp/1973753677/ref=pd_bxgy_img_3/141-1543337-0163153?_encoding=UTF8&pd_rd_i=1973753677&pd_rd_r=2e475da2-03c1-4a59-8bdb-078e0a1741f7&pd_rd_w=ZZqiE&pd_rd_wg=LCvkS&pf_rd_p=f325d01c-4658-4593-be83-3e12ca663f0e&pf_rd_r=NBHJZ2AQS0Y516FZXCGY&psc=1&refRID=NBHJZ2AQS0Y516FZXCGY

https://www.brightmachines.com/

https://www.vicarious.com/solutions

https://covariant.ai/solutions

https://research.aimultiple.com/ai-stats/#healthcare

https://www.crunchbase.com/organization/andreessen-horowitz

https://www.bluejeans.com/use-cases/education

https://tandem.chat/

https://www.bluescape.com/

https://slab.com/

SEA CHANGE, DO CHANGE

https://www.starship.xyz/business/

https://www.manna.aero/

ABOUT THE AUTHOR

Frank Dappah is a serial entrepreneur, author and investor. Frank has written various books on topics like Marketing, social media, entrepreneurship and other areas of business. Frank resides in Charlotte, North Carolina with his business partner/wife, Bernice.

SEA CHANGE, DO CHANGE

OTHER TITLES

Customer Journeys: Why every Startup needs a Customer Advisory Board.

What happens when you listen to your customers? What happens when you build a customer-centric startup? - One that is intricately connected to its customers and all the men and women whose lives are impacted every day by your products and services?

STATUS UPDATE

Strategic social media marketing can be the cure-all your business needs to reach the right audience at the right time. STATUS UPDATE is an easy-to-digest guide to help any Life and/or Health agent or agency make the most of their Facebook marketing system.

'STATUS UPDATE' is a must-read for any Insurance Agency owner or Broker looking for unique ideas on how to get the most out of their Facebook marketing –

How to generate and convert health and life insurance sales leads with Facebook Ads

FRANK DAPPAH

Small business social media marketing guide

CONTINUOUS CONNECTIVITY: Leveraging the power of text messaging to grow your business and enhance your brand reach.

I have always considered Sales and Marketing to be that which is most vital to the Startup success and growth of any organization - both at the for profit and nonprofit level. You can have the best ice cream, or coffee in town.

FRANK DAPPAH
AUTHOR OF *STARTUP MONDAY*

Leveraging the power of text messaging to grow your business and enhance your brand reach

Find these and many other titles from the author at Amazon.com, Ostrichpress.com, or wherever you buy books.

SEA CHANGE, DO CHANGE

OSTRICH®

Ostrich Publishers

We love books! It is in our DNA. It is the food we eat and the air we breathe.

We are working hard to build an all-inclusive publishing and distribution platform.

Our Mission

OSTRICH is an all-digital publisher. Our mission is to create a robust medium through which talented independent Authors and Creatives can share their works with the rest of the world.

What We Do

As part of our overall mission, we work closely with authors of all backgrounds to help bring their works to life. Through our robust distribution infrastructure, we can help Authors, who would otherwise go unnoticed, to plan, create and distribute their finished products worldwide. We work with Authors at every step of the process, from brainstorming, to writing, to distribution and marketing. We are working hard to build an all-inclusive publishing and distribution platform.

OSTRICH Publishers (https://www.ostrichpress.com/)

SEA CHANGE, DO CHANGE

SEA CHANGE
DO CHANGE

FRANK DAPPAH

OSTRICH

Ostrich Press LLC. www.ostrichpress.com

SEA CHANGE, DO CHANGE

Copyright © 2012 Ostrich press

All rights reserved.

ISBN: 9798722754752

SEA CHANGE, DO CHANGE

SEA CHANGE DO CHANGE

Discussing the world of equity crowdfunding, Innovation, and entrepreneurship in the era of COVID

FRANK DAPPAH
Author of Startup Monday & Goals Inc.

SEA CHANGE, DO CHANGE

SEA CHANGE, DO CHANGE

SEA CHANGE, DO CHANGE

www.ingramcontent.com/pod-product-compliance
Lightning Source LLC
Chambersburg PA
CBHW020426220526
45464CB00002B/590